DATE DUE

	NOV 1 2	OC 28 '04	
NOV 1	JAN 2 7		
APR 1 8	MAR 1 6		
'86	OCT 2 7		
SEP 26 86	OCT 2 1		
OCT 1 '86	NOV 2		
OCT 17 '86	DEC 1 7		
OCT 29 '86	APR 1 8		
NOV 5 '86	NOV 0 7 1994		
FEB 27	NOV 2	A.M.	
DEC 0 4	NOV 3	A.M.	
SEP 29	NOV 2 0 1996		
SEP 29	NOV 3 0 1996		
DEC 2 0	OCT 1 6 1997		
MAY 1 4	JAN 2 2 1998		
MAY 2 4	3-3-99		
OCT 0 7	APR 0 9 1999		
NOV 5	APR 2 3 1999		
GAYLORD			PRINTED IN U.S.A.

RACING CARS

The Rourke Guides are a series of scientific and technical books. All measurements are shown in the Metric System. This is the system the scientific community uses world wide. A small conversion chart below will help those not familiar with the system.

In addition, we, the publishers have listed European terminology with American equivalents.

Metric System Conversion Chart

Unit		U.S. Equivalent	
millimetre, millimeter	(mm)	.039	inch
centimetre, centimeter	(cm)	.39	inch
metre, meter	(m)	39.4	inches
kilometre, kilometer	(km)	.62	mile
gram	(g)	15.4	grains
kilogram	(kg)	2.2	pounds
litre, liter	(l)	1.05	quarts
cubic centimetre, centimeter	(cc)	.061	cubic inch
tonne, ton	(tn)	2000	pounds

Terminology Aid

colour	—	color	queued	—	lined up
tonne	—	ton	RPM	—	revolutions per minute
defence	—	defense	stabilise	—	stabilize
armour	—	armor	organise	—	organize
aeroplane	—	airplane	fulfil	—	fulfill
centre	—	center	customise	—	customize
calibre	—	caliber	£, pound	—	$2.00
favour	—	favor	honour	—	honor
manoeuvre	—	maneuver	valour	—	valor
programme	—	program	sledges	—	sleds
BHP	—	braking horse power	ploughshares	—	plowshares (blade of plow)
tyre	—	tire	invalided out	—	medical discharge
petrol	—	gasoline	labour	—	labor
neighbour	—	neighbor	odours	—	odor
harbour	—	harbor	fibres	—	fibers
practise	—	practice	neutralise	—	neutralize
amphitheatre	—	amphitheater			

RACING CARS

8782

by Kevin Desmond

Illustrated by Jim Dugdale

THE ROURKE CORPORATION
Windermere, Florida

The frontispiece shows Stirling Moss in the Vanwall leading Mike Hawthorn in the Ferrari in the Moroccan Grand Prix of 1958.

The author wishes to acknowledge the kind assistance of Cyril Posthumus, David Tremayne and David Muir.

©1982 The Rourke Corporation, Inc.

Published by Granada Publishing 1981
Copyright ©Granada

Published by The Rourke Corporation, Inc., P.O. Box 711, Windermere, Florida 32786. Copyright ©1982 by The Rourke Corporation, Inc. All copyrights reserved. No part of this book may be reproduced in any form without written permission from the publisher. Printed in the United States of America.

Library of Congress Cataloging in Publication Data

Desmond, Kevin.
  Racing cars.

  (Rourke guide)
  Includes index.
  Summary: Text and drawings highlight the features
and developments of Grand Prix entrants from the
first race held in France in 1906 to the world-wide
circuits of today.
  1. Automobiles, Racing—Juvenile literature.
[1. Automobiles, Racing—History] I. Dugdale,
Jim, 1960-   ill.   II. Title.   III. Series.
TL236.D47   1982   629.2'28   82-10184
ISBN 0-86592-757-X

Contents

High Beginnings

Whose motor car is fastest? When our great grandfathers first asked that challenging question over 80 years ago, they were talking about tall, crude vehicles, built of wood and steel. Their cars were powered by deep, grumbling engines of 13 litres' capacity, which developed 135 horsepower at 1400 rpm (revolutions per minute). The brave drivers and riding mechanics wore protective leather clothing. Crouching down, they accelerated to almost 100 mph. Wrestling with the controls they would try to overtake their rivals on the open roads.

The Austro-Hungarian driver, Ferenc Szisz, stands beside the 13-litre Renault, in which he and his mechanic Marceau (seated) won the 1906 French Grand Prix.

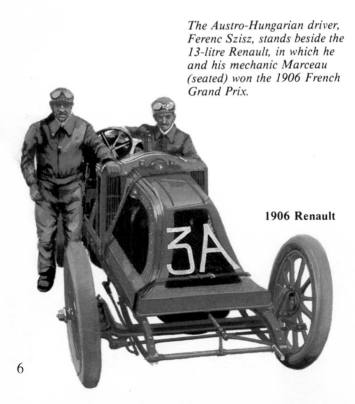

1906 Renault

6

Today, when we ask the same question, we have in mind vehicles of a very different nature. In a lifetime racing cars have been made half their weight, four times as powerful and twice as fast. Today's cars are built of metal alloys and plastics. Some have high-whining engines of three litres' capacity, developing some 480 brake horsepower (bhp) at 12,200 rpm. Others have only 1½-litre engines but, with turbocharging, can develop as much as 550 bhp at 11,500 rpm. Their pilot wears fire-proof asbestos clothing, and a hardened plastic crash helmet. Climbing down into his rear-engined car, he drives at a lightning 180 mph down the track, cornering at 160 mph, lying almost flat on his back!

Elio de Angelis, the Italian driver, prepares to climb down into Colin Chapman's Essex-Lotus 81, which he raced during 1980 and 1981.

1981 Essex-Lotus 81

Racing Begins

The first steamcar races took place over a century ago in America and France. Then, in 1895, petrol-engined cars came into their own. A race was held in France from Paris to Bordeaux and back, a distance of 1178 kilometres. The first to finish was Emile Levassor, a 51-year-old Frenchman. He was driving a Panhard-Levassor, powered by a 1.2-litre German Daimler engine, developing 3½ hp. Driving the whole distance on his own, he steered his craft over the bumpy roads with a

1895 Panhard-Levassor

tiller, as if it were a boat. His time of 48 hours 47 minutes gave Monsieur Levassor an average speed of 15 mph!

At that time, motor races had to be run from city to city, because nobody had yet built a special circuit. But within five years, the most successful cars, the French Panhards, were achieving speeds of 50-60 mph. When some drivers were killed during races, efforts were made to ensure greater safety. This concern continues today.

Emile Levassor and his 'horse-less carriage' are welcomed back to Paris. Of the 22 starters only nine finished and some were several hours behind the others!

Plenty of Litres

In 1906, the French Automobile Club held the first Grand Prix race on a 64-mile road circuit near Le Mans. The French words, Grand Prix (meaning big prize), were used because the winner would receive a great deal of prize money. Although the weight of the racing cars was limited by the rules, the engine capacity was not. The capacity of the 130 hp Panhard engine was 18.2 litres, while the Dufaux engine with only 4 cylinders was 26.4 litres. By this time, manufacturers had begun to lower the height of their cars from the ground. The driver and his mechanic no longer sat on top of the cars, but were positioned lower down inside the cockpit.

The 1907 Grand Prix was held on a 48-mile road circuit near Dieppe in France. For the first time, long holes, or pits, were dug by the roadside, where cars could stop to change tyres and refuel. Even today, racing cars still come in to the pits.

1908 Mercedes

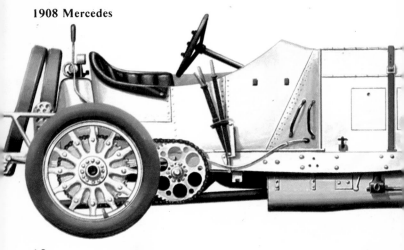

The French Mors which Henry Fournier drove to win the Paris-Berlin race of 1901. Notice the chain-drive system.

1907 Fiat

Italian driver Felice Nazzaro's 1907 Fiat had a 16.3-litre overhead valve engine developing 130 bhp at 1600 rpm. Nazzaro won the French Grand Prix, averaging 70 mph for 6¾ hours.

From 1907, each nation raced with different coloured cars: Italian red, French blue, British green, German white (or silver). Christian Lautenschlager drove his 12.8 litre Mercédès at over 100 mph to win the 1908 French Grand Prix for Germany.

11

The Coming of Science

In 1906 a scientifically-designed motor-racing circuit, measuring 4.4 kilometres (over 2½ miles) in circumference, was built in Surrey, England. It was called Brooklands Motor Course. Using its steep concrete bankings, British car manufacturers, such as Sunbeam and Vauxhall, could test their ideas at high speeds, and improve their cars' design and performance. Later on, similar enclosed tracks were built in America, France, Italy and Spain. For Grand Prix racing cars, the days of the open road were numbered.

Following the defeat of their cars by the Italian Fiat in 1907 and the German Mercédès in 1908, French manufacturers and the Automobile Club of France

Georges Boillot in the 1912 Peugeot is pursued by a British 3-litre Sunbeam, designed by Louis Coatelen.

1912 Peugeot

decided not to hold any Grand Prix races for a number of years. Racing, they said, was too expensive.

When the Grand Prix was revived in 1912, it brought with it a breakthrough in engine design, especially in the Peugeot. Its 130 hp engine was of only 7.6 litres' capacity. But it had special twin overhead camshafts to operate the 16 valves, and higher rpms. It was mounted on a much lighter framework – or chassis. These innovations, largely developed by a 27-year-old engineer called Ernest Henry, gave the Peugeot drivers the greater control at higher speeds that they needed to win races. In 1912 and 1913, the Peugeots were unbeatable!

1912 Sunbeam

The German Onslaught

For the 1914 Grand Prix, cars were limited to only 4.5 litres. Fourteen manufacturers had entered with 41 cars between them. Almost all were equipped with the overhead camshaft. While the favourite was Georges Boillot in Henry's latest Peugeot, the Germans appeared with a revolutionary Mercédès. Since their 1908 victory, the Mercédès factory at Stuttgart had been developing lightweight aeroplane engines. The engine they fitted into their five new Grand Prix cars owed much to this. It gave 115 bhp at 3200 rpm. This meant that the whole car, weighing only 2380 pounds, about 1000 kilograms, was capable of a top speed of 115 mph.

Christian Lautenschlager in the victorious 1914 Mercédès. Its V-shaped radiator created less wind resistance – and greater speeds.

1914 Mercédès

The Grand Prix course was 20 laps of a hilly 38-kilometre circuit near Lyons in France. With great care, the German drivers examined the road conditions, practised taking the corners in touring cars, and planned their pit stops. The over-confident French drivers returning from racing in America on the evening before the race had no time to prepare.

Watched by 300,000 cheering people, Georges Boillot drove the race of his life in the Peugeot. But the Germans were too fast for him. Two laps before the finish, Lautenschlager overtook him. Soon after, the Peugeot broke down, and was overtaken by the Mercédès cars of Wagner and Salzer. This gave the Germans a 1-2-3 victory, the first in Grand Prix history. Bitterly disappointed, Boillot had to be helped from his car, weeping. Three weeks later Europe was at war and Mercédès aero engines were being used in aerial combat biplanes.

The Roaring Twenties

While Europe was at war, the Americans continued to enjoy motor racing, testing new cars at Indianapolis and elsewhere. They developed their cars, taking full advantage of European aero-engine research. Then they too were drawn into the war.

After the war the Europeans made every effort to catch up with the Americans. In 1919 Ernest Henry hastily designed a new French car for Ernest Ballot, to compete against the Americans in their Indianapolis 500-mile race. These Ballots had straight 8-cylinder engines. Although fastest, they lost the race through wheel and mechanical troubles. But the 8-cylinder engines now became popular. When the French Grand Prix was revived in 1921, it was held on a new 17.2 kilometre circuit at Le Mans. The Americans adopted the European capacity limitation of three litres, but still came first.

Grand Prix racing was no longer limited to France. There were soon Italian, Spanish, Belgian, British and German Grands Prix. Between 1922 and 1925 the capacity limitation was further reduced, to two litres. During these years the Italian Fiat 804 and 805 cars were victorious, and also the British Sunbeams.

Malcolm Lockheed's hydraulic braking system enabled Jimmy Murphy's Duesenberg to average 78 mph for 322 miles during the 1921 French Grand Prix.

16   **1921 Duesenberg**

Felice Nazzaro won the 1922 French Grand Prix at Strasbourg in this 2-litre six-cylinder Fiat 804.

1922 Fiat 804

The revolutionary Benz Tropfenwagens (Teardrop cars) had their engine behind the driver. Three of them competed in the 1923 Italian Grand Prix but all failed to win.

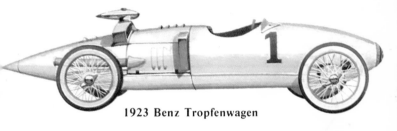

1923 Benz Tropfenwagen

Englishman Henry Segrave drove this 2-litre Sunbeam, 'a Fiat in green paint', to victory in the 1923 French Grand Prix at Tours.

1923 Sunbeam

17

The Fated Champion

Nicola Romeo, owner of the Alfa-Romeo car company of Milan, desperately wanted a Grand Prix winner. So he persuaded one of Fiat's successful designers, young Vittorio Jano, to work for him. Jano designed a racing car with a supercharged straight-8-cylinder engine, developing 140 bhp at 5500 rpm. The car became known as the P2. With Antonio Ascari driving, the first Alfa-Romeo P2 reached a top speed of 121.16 mph along a 6.2-mile road at Cremona.

In 1924, the P2s won the French and Italian Grands Prix from their French rivals, the Delages and the

Bugattis. They won the 1925 European Grand Prix in Belgium. But in the French Grand Prix at the banked concrete Montlhéry circuit, Antonio Ascari was leading, when one of his wheels caught the wooden fence, ripping it up and overturning. Fortunately, riding mechanics had been banned from Grand Prix cars that year, so only Antonio Ascari was killed. But it was a tragic loss for Italy. Although the other P2s were withdrawn from that race, P2s came in 1st, 2nd and 5th at the International Grand Prix at Monza, Italy. Soon after, Alfa-Romeo were awarded the first official World Championship.

Antonio Ascari, the Alfa-Romeo P2 champion driver, had strongly complained of the dangers of the wooden fence around the Montlhéry circuit. His complaints were ignored, and the result was his tragic death.

1925 Alfa-Romeo P2

Beautiful Bugattis

The big motor car manufacturers had gone into Grand Prix racing so that people would buy their ordinary cars. In the late 1920s, with larger numbers of cars on the road, some companies decided to stop building Grand Prix cars; it was an unnecessary expense for them. But Italian-born French artist Ettore Bugatti was not concerned with cost.

In 1924 Bugatti designed and built his Bugatti Type 35. This was powered by a 2-litre straight-8 engine, developing 95 hp at 5000 rpm. The car weighed only 1690 pounds (766 kilograms) empty. It steered beautifully and accelerated to over 110 mph. Immediately successful, Bugatti decided that he would sell as many

1924 Bugatti

Type 35s as possible. Whoever was rich enough, could own a Bugatti.

From 1924 to 1926, Bugattis won over 1000 races. In 1927 they won 806 races including several Grands Prix! As the Grand Prix capacity limitation was further lowered in 1926 to 1½ litres, Bugatti produced the Type 39. This was a supercharged engine developing 110 bhp at 5300 rpm. Together with the slightly different Bugatti Types B, C and T, all these cars were popular and successful.

The distinctive horseshoe radiator and alloy-spoked wheels of the 1924 Bugatti 35. Sometimes the first six places in a race would be taken by Bugattis. The secrets of success were a better tuned engine, better prepared car, and greater driving skills.

Speed Kid Demon

The most famous race circuit in the United States of America was Indianapolis in the State of Indiana. It was designed as a rectangle, with curved corners. Because the track surface was built of bricks, Indianapolis Motor Speedway was often nicknamed 'The Brickyard'. Other American tracks were built of wooden planks. The most important race at 'Indy' was run each year over a distance of 500 miles.

In the 1920s, Duesenberg racing cars took it in turns with Miller-engined cars to win the Indy. Like Bugatti in Europe, Harry A. Miller from Los Angeles sold his racing cars to whoever had enough money to buy them. But because they were so beautifully designed and

1926 Miller 91

built, they were very expensive. From 1926 to 1929, the American capacity limitation was also 1½ litres. So Harry Miller and Leo Goossen produced their 91 racing car (91 cubic inches equal 1½ litres, hence the name). Its engine developed 154 bhp at 7200 rpm.

Like the Bugatti 35, the Miller 91 was immensely successful. In 1926, Frank Lockhart, aged only 23, won the Indy 500, driving a Miller 91. The following year, they improved the car even further so that it reached 140 mph on the race circuits. They even tuned a Miller 91 engine to develop 285 bhp at over 8000 rpm. To top that, they filled the tank with special fuel and Frank Lockhart drove the 'Special' up and down the dried-up Lake Muroc in California. It reached an amazing top speed of 171 mph and Lockhart was nicknamed the Speed Kid Demon.

Frank Lockhart in the 1½-litre Miller 91, in which he won the 1926 Indianapolis 500 race.

The Concrete Saucer

Brooklands Motor Course, the home of the British Grand Prix for two years, was the scene of many exciting battles. English racing cars, with their amateur drivers, were subject to a handicapping system. This meant that the slower a car was, the bigger start it was given, so that all cars might finish together in a fairer and more exciting race.

Two Delages race round the bumpy Byfleet Banking, Brooklands Motor Course, during the 1927 British Grand Prix.

1927 Delage

In 1926, Albert Lory designed a new 1½-litre engine for his very wealthy French employer, Louis Delage. Running smoothly on ball bearings, it had twin super-chargers and developed 170 bhp at 8000 rpm. This gave it a top speed of 130 mph.

In 1927, Delages won the British Grand Prix at Brooklands, averaging 86 mph, as well as the French, Spanish and European.

The Furious Thirties

The early 1930s saw no limit on litre capacity. Instead, races must last less than 10 hours in 1931, then less than 5 hours in 1932. In 1931 Ettore Bugatti produced a new car. This was the 2.3-litre Type 51 Bugatti with twin overhead camshaft. Once again, Bugatti 51s began to win the major races, against competition from the 2.5-litre straight-8 Maserati cars.

Then Benito Mussolini, Italy's dictator, decided that, to impress Europe, only Italian cars must win Grands Prix. He pumped money into Alfa-Romeo so that they might produce an unbeatable racing car. Once again, Vittorio Jano put on his thinking cap and designed the P3 Alfa-Romeo Monoposto. Monoposto means central single-seater. With only one seat, the car could be narrower and faster. With a twin-supercharged 2.6-litre engine, developing 215 bhp at 5600 rpm, the P3 Alfa-Romeo Monoposto proved almost unbeatable at 140 mph. Brilliantly driven by Tazio Nuvolari, Rudolf Caracciola, Luigi Fagioli and Louis Chiron, the P3s fully satisfied Mussolini.

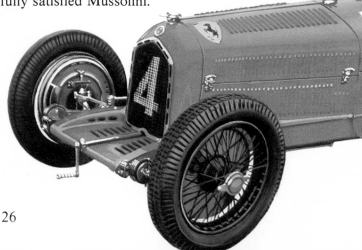

1932 Bugatti Type 51

Influenced by the American Miller 91, Bugatti Type 51s, built at Molsheim, near Strasbourg, had twin overhead camshafts.

1930 Maserati 6C

In 1925, the brothers Alfieri and Ernesto Maserati produced their Diatto racing car. In 1926 they appeared with the 1½-litre straight-8 Maserati. By 1930, they had progressed to this 2½-litre Maserati 6C.

1932 Alfa-Romeo P3

The Alfa-Romeo P3, with its twin supercharged 2.6-litre engine, developing 215 bhp at 5,600 rpm, maintained unbeatable speeds of 140 mph or more.

The German Revival

In 1934, a new Grand Prix Formula was introduced. Racing cars must not weigh more than 750 kilograms (1650 pounds). Out of this limitation came two very famous and successful cars.

The four Maserati brothers – Alfieri, Bindo, Ernesto and Ettore – built cars in Bologna in Italy. In 1933, the slim Maserati 8CM was developed. Powered by a 210-bhp engine, it had four hydraulically-operated brakes. At high speed, the 8CM was very difficult to control. Tazio Nuvolari, one of the greatest racing drivers of all time, scored several successes with his Maserati 8CM in 1934, but he also crashed in it.

1935 Mercedes W35

Elsewhere Adolf Hitler, the leader of Nazi Germany, decided that German – not Italian – cars must win the great Grands Prix. So he offered an irresistible sum of money for the racing car that could win the most races in the 750-kilogram class. Mercédès-Benz developed their streamlined W25 car with a 3.3-litre engine giving 314 bhp at 5800 rpm. Especially light metals were used in the bodywork and all four wheels had independent suspension. Auto Union, a combination of four car manufacturers, produced an extraordinary car. Instead of its 16-cylinder 4.4-litre engine being in front of the driver, the Auto Union engine was behind him. This was the idea of Dr Ferdinand Porsche. At first everybody laughed at the idea of a rear-engined car, but then the Auto Unions began to win Grands Prix. Before long, the Alfa-Romeo P3s, Bugatti 51s and Maserati 8CMs had been left behind. In 1934, Mercédès won four races and Hitler's prize money. Auto Union won three.

1935 Maserati 8CM

Philippe Etancelin in the Maserati 8CM in pursuit of Rudolf Caracciola in the Mercédès W35 during the 1935 Monaco Grand Prix.

Total Power

Seven wins in one year was not enough for the Nazis –
they must win every race – no expense spared. In 1935
Mercédès-Benz produced the W25B – 3.9 litres
developing 430 bhp. With a top speed of 175mph, it won
nine Grands Prix. In 1936 Auto Union developed their
Type C – 6 litres developing 520 bhp. Also a Grand Prix
winner, it had a top speed of 190 mph! Next came
Mercédès-Benz with the W125, the most powerful car
ever built. It had a 5.7-litre engine which gave 550 bhp at
5800 rpm and a speed of 185mph.

The victorious German drivers, Bernd Rosemeyer,
Rudolf Caracciola and Hans Stuck amongst others, had
to be brave as well as skilful to control these monsters,
especially on the corners. They would slide them round
at 100mph.

*The perfection of total power came in 1939 with the Mercédès-Benz
W154, which gave Hermann Lang victory in the Swiss Grand Prix.*

1939 Mercédès-Benz W154

1938 Auto Union Type D

The Auto Union Type D was driven by the masterful Tazio Nuvolari to victory in the 1938 British Grand Prix.

From 1938, there was a new Grand Prix Formula, limited to either 3-litre supercharged cars — or 4.5-litre unsupercharged cars. The weight limit was 850 kilograms (1870 pounds). Both Mercédès-Benz and Auto Union built 3-litre V12 engines, which revved at over 7000 rpm. Although these engines — the W154 and Type D — were half the size of the 1934-37 engines, the cars were just as fast and successful. Even Italy's Tazio Nuvolari drove for Auto Union.

The Germans were not the only ones to produce successful cars during the 1930s. In 1934 two Englishmen, Raymond Mays and Peter Berthon, produced the ERA (English Racing Automobile). This was a single-seater car with a 6-cylinder 1½-litre supercharged engine. During the next five years, some eighteen ERAs were built in Lincolnshire – Types A, B, C, D, and E. With such drivers as Prince Bira of Thailand and Raymond Mays, the ERAs were extremely successful in smaller class racing.

In 1938, the Maserati brothers developed a 3-litre, straight-8-cylinder engine, giving 350 bhp at over 6000 rpm. This powered the Maserati 8CTF. Although they were unable to beat the German cars in Europe, one 8CTF went out to Indianapolis. With Wilbur Shaw driving, it won the Indy 500 in both 1939 and 1940, easily beating the Miller-designed, Offenhauser-engined cars. The Americans immediately starting copying the Maserati shape.

1935 ERA Type B

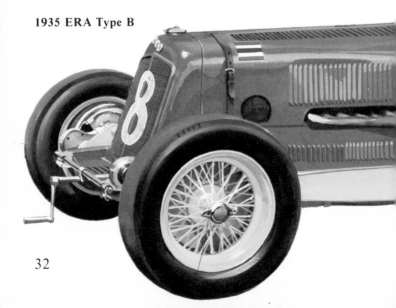

1939 Maserati 8CTF

Wilbur Shaw in the Boyle Special, the Maserati 8CTF in which he averaged 114mph to win the Indy 500 race in 1939 and 1940.

His Royal Highness Prince Birabongse and his cousin, Prince Chula, raced two famous ERA cars: they called them Romulus and Remus after the famous twin brothers of Ancient Rome. This is Romulus.

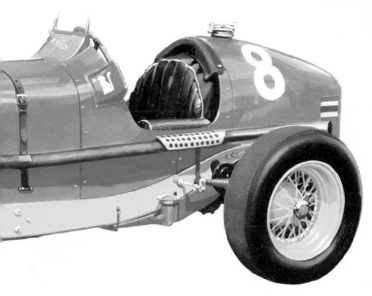

33

Exit the Supercharger

1952 Ferrari Type 500

After the war, the new Grand Prix Formula was for 1½-litre supercharged or 4½-litre unsupercharged cars. The Maserati factory improved their 1½-litre supercharged pre-war car into the 4CLT/48. Winning its first race at San Remo, the 4CLT/48 was christened the San Remo Maserati. With twin superchargers, the Alfa-Romeo Type 158 had soon been developed to give 420 bhp at 9600 rpm and renamed Type 159. Driving Alfa-Romeos, Dr Nino Farina won the 1950 World Championship and Juan Fangio from Argentina won the 1951 Championship.

Supercharged racing cars had been totally successful since the 1920s. But in 1951 Enzo Ferrari and his brilliant designer, Aurelio Lampredi, created a revolutionary, unsupercharged 4.5-litre Ferrari. Driven by Gigi Villoresi and Alberto Ascari, the quieter new Ferraris soon proved the supercharged Maserati 4CLT/48 and Alfa-Romeo 158/159 out of date.

The Grand Prix Formula was next changed to allow 2-litre cars. Superbly driven by Alberto Ascari, the 4-cylinder twin overhead camshaft Ferrari Type 500 won the World Championships of 1952 and 1953.

34

Alberto Ascari in the Ferrari Type 500, in which he won two World Championships and 20 Grands Prix. The son of Antonio Ascari, Alberto never raced without his lucky blue helmet.

The 4CLT/48 Maserati had a tubular framework chassis. After the Maserati brothers had sold their business to the Orsi family, they went away and developed the less successful OSCA racing car.

1948 Maserati 4CLT/48

The Alfa-Romeo 158/159, designed by Gioacchino Colombo, was so compact for its power that it was nicknamed the Alfetta, meaning Little Alfa.

1950 Alfa-Romeo 158/159

The German Comeback

In 1954, the Germans returned to Grand Prix racing with the Mercédès-Benz W196. Its straight-8-cylinder 2.5-litre engine was fuel-injected. It gave 290 bhp at 8500 rpm and was fitted into the front of a lightweight streamlined body. Each wheel was given independent suspension using twisting or 'torsion' bars. At over 150 mph, the W196s were easy Grand Prix winners. They were driven by Fangio, Moss, Kling and Hermann.

Only Lancia's first Grand Prix car, the D50, threatened the Mercédès. Vittorio Jano, designer of the

Juan Fangio in the Mercédès W196 leads Alberto Ascari in the Lancia V8 during the 1955 Monaco Grand Prix. Ascari later crashed into the sea – but survived, only to die four days later.

1955 Mercédès W196

Alfa-Romeo P2 and P3, created a V8-cylinder engine and fitted it at an angle as part of the chassis. Instead of placing the fuel tanks at the back, he placed them on either side.

In early 1955, the Lancia D50 threatened the Mercédès W196 for the World Championship. Then two terrible tragedies occurred. Lancia driver Alberto Ascari was killed testing a sportscar. Then a Mercédès sportscar crashed in a race at Le Mans, killing over 80 people. Both Lancia and Mercédès-Benz withdrew from Grand Prix racing.

1955 Lancia V8

British Beginnings

In the 1950s, Tony Vandervell, a British motor-racing enthusiast, decided that it was about time the British beat the Italians. With money made from his Thinwall bearings business, Vandervell began to pay for the development of a Grand Prix car. He started off with a modified Ferrari called the Thinwall Special. From its success, the Vanwall was created. With special fuel injection, the 4-cylinder 2.5-litre Vanwall engine developed 285 bhp, and was slowed by superior disc brakes.

In 1957 Stirling Moss drove a Vanwall to win the British Grand Prix. This was the first time since 1924 that an Englishman had won a major Grand Prix in an English car. In 1958, a new Championship was introduced for racing car constructors. By winning six Grands Prix, Vanwalls became the first to win the Constructors Championship.

At the same time, wealthy young Kenneth MacAlpine went racing with his Connaught car team. MacAlpine was never as successful as Vandervell, although in 1955 a Connaught Type B won the Syracuse Grand Prix in Sicily. Both Vanwall and Connaught teams may have had short careers. But they showed the beginnings of British success in Grand Prix racing.

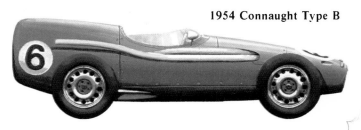

1954 Connaught Type B

The first Connaught Type B to appear at the start of the 1954 Season was nicknamed the 'toothpaste tube'. It owed much to aircraft design.

The 1956 Vanwall had a lightweight tubular framework chassis, scientifically designed by Colin Chapman. Its streamlined bodywork was designed by Chapman's friend, Frank Costin, who had once worked for the de Havilland aircraft company. Costin created curved aerodynamic shapes to allow the air to flow more easily past the car. From now on, aerodynamics were crucial in racing car development.

1956 Vanwall

Mid-engined Victory

From 1954 to 1957, a fleet of Maserati 250Fs, with their 2½-litre 6-cylinder engines in front, won over 34 major races. Fangio, the great Argentinian, won one of his five World Championships driving the 250F. For 1958, Maserati had developed an even more powerful V12 engine. But they had to pull out of Grand Prix racing because of lack of money. That year, Enzo Ferrari produced the V6-cylinder front-engined 'Dino', named after his son who had just died. The 2½-litre Ferrari Dino gave Englishman Mike Hawthorn the 1958 World Championship.

The Maserati 250F, in which Fangio won his fifth World Championship and his greatest race: the 1957 German Grand Prix at the Nurburgring.

1957 Maserati 250F

1957 Ferrari Dino

The Ferrari Dino, in which Mike Hawthorn won the 1958 French Grand Prix at 125.4 mph, and also the World Championship.

Meanwhile, Charles Cooper and his son John had pioneered a racing car where the 2½-litre Coventry Climax engine was, once again, behind the driver. With this Cooper-Climax T51, Australian Jack Brabham won the 1959 and 1960 World Drivers and Constructors Championships. After that, everyone built mid-engined racing cars.

The Cooper-Climax T51, in which Australian Jack Brabham won the 1959 World Championshp, had bolt-on alloy wheels and disc brakes.

1959 Cooper-Climax T51

The Swinging Sixties

Before the war, Raymond Mays and Peter Berthon had produced the successful ERA. In the late 1940s, they began British Racing Motors (BRM). Paid for by British Industry, the first front-engined BRM racing cars, their V-16 engines revving at 11,000, were a noisy failure. Soon after, a motor industrialist, Sir Alfred Owen, took over the funding of the BRM project. During the late 1950s several BRMs appeared, including the P25, its

1962 BRM

The P56 began the 1962 season with the nickname 'Stackpipe BRM' because of the exhaust pipe design. But the exhausts regularly came loose and were soon replaced by these less dangerous, shorter pipes.

42

2.5-litre engine developing 272 bhp at 8500 rpm. Despite continual modification, the cars were not a great success, and the rear-engined P48 was no better. People used to laugh at BRMs.

In 1961, the Grand Prix Formula was changed to 1½ litres. Sir Alfred Owen told the BRM team that unless they came up with two Grand Prix wins, he would stop paying their bills. Tony Rudd designed a V8 engine developing 188 bhp at 10,500 rpm. This was fitted into the BRM P56. In 1962, not only did English driver Graham Hill drive the BRM P56 to win the World Drivers Championship, but BRM won the Constructors Championship as well. Sir Alfred Owen was satisfied and the laughing stopped.

The Flying Scot

In competition with BRM cars, for 14 years, brilliant designer Colin Chapman worked to develop his low, lightweight racing cars. Though enjoyable, this work often made him and his team too tired to stay awake, just as the tasty fruit of the lotus plant can also make you sleepy. For this reason, Chapman called his racing cars, Lotus. His first rear-engined car was the Lotus 18.

In Lotus cars, instead of sitting up, drivers lie back with their feet between the front wheels. In 1962 Chapman produced the Lotus 25. Instead of its chassis

1963 Lotus 25

being constructed of a complicated tubular framework, the Lotus 25 chassis was one aluminium shell, riveted together. Into this 'Monocoque' chassis, Chapman fitted the Coventry-Climax V8 engine. The Lotus 25 was so successful that before very long everyone had copied the monocoque design.

Lotus 25 driver Jim Clark just failed to beat BRM P56 driver Graham Hill to the 1962 World Championship. But in 1963 the Coventry-Climax V8 was made more powerful by fuel-injection. Jim Clark, 'the Flying Scot', and his Lotus 25 became the first ever to win 12 Grands Prix and both World Championships.

Jim Clark averaged 132 mph in the Lotus 25 to win both the 1962 and 1963 Belgian Grands Prix at Spa Francorchamps.

"Nothing Else" Cars

Some cars only win one Grand Prix. Soichiro Honda's motorcycles, built in Tokyo, Japan, were unbeatable. So Honda decided to build a Japanese Grand Prix racing car. He used a 1½-litre V12 motorcycle-influenced engine. This developed 230 bhp at an amazing 11,000 rpm. It was mounted transversely – or across – the back of the car. Driving the Honda RA 272 with great skill, Richie Ginther won the Mexican Grand Prix at the end of 1965 – and nothing else.

In 1966, to make racing more exciting the Grand Prix litre capacity formula was increased to 3 litres again. Dan Gurney, an American, paid the British Weslake Engineering Company to build a 3-litre V12 engine for his Anglo-American racing team. Driving the Eagle-Weslake, Gurney won the 1967 Belgian Grand Prix – and nothing else.

A 3-litre H-16-cylinder engine, developing 400 bhp at 10,500 rpm, was installed in the BRM P83. In 1966, a Lotus with the BRM H-16 engine won the United States Grand Prix – and nothing else.

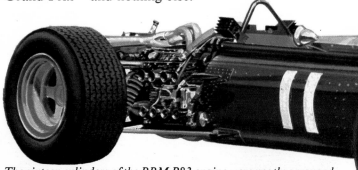

The sixteen cylinders of the BRM P83 engine were neatly arranged in an H-shape lying on its side. With the gearbox, they became part of the monocoque aluminium chassis.

1964 Honda RA 272

After Californian Richie Ginther's victorious Honda had used
Goodyear tyres – a tyre war began amongst Dunlop, Goodyear and
Firestone for top Grand Prix honours.

1966 Eagle-Weslake

Dan Gurney's V12 Eagle-Weslake raced under American colours.
But both chassis – almost a copy of Len Terry's Lotus 38 – and
engine, designed by Aubrey Woods, were built in Britain.

1966 BRM P83

Down Under On Top

In 1960, Australian driver Jack Brabham teamed up with his friend Ron Tauranac to build his own racing cars. In 1966, they took an Australian Repco V8 engine and installed it at the back of their BT 19 (Brabham-Tauranac). For the first time in Grand Prix racing, Jack Brabham won not only the World Drivers Championship but also the Constructors Championship, driving a car which he had co-designed and built with Ron Tauranac. The following year, 1967, Brabham-Repco won both Championships, this time with New Zealander

The wings-on-stilts helped the Brabham-Repco BT26 to corner but were a danger to driver and spectators alike. This one fortunately only buckled – but it might have flown off into the crowd.

1968 Brabham Repco BT26

Denny Hulme at the wheel, first of the BT20, then the BT24.

For 1968, Brabham and Tauranac came up with the BT26. It used a more powerful 4-cam Repco engine and two wings on stilts. Some racing cars already had one wing at the back, but this was the first time two wings had been used. Although these wings helped the BT26 in cornering at high speed, there was a danger of them snapping off. For this reason the Grand Prix authorities banned them. The 4-cam Repco engine had no success, so it was replaced by a reliable new engine: the 3-litre V8 Ford-Cosworth DFV.

The Cosworth Revolution

In 1967, Colin Chapman brought his revolutionary Lotus-Ford 49 to the race circuits. This was designed around the Ford-Cosworth DFV-8 engine for the 3-litre Formula. It was called the Cosworth because it was designed by two ex-Lotus engineers, Mike *Cos*tin and Keith Duck*worth*. Its development was paid for by the Ford company at Dagenham. It gave over 400 bhp at over 9000 rpm. Using its lightweight cylinder block, Chapman and Maurice Phillipe designed the monocoque Lotus 49. Driven by Jim Clark, the Lotus 49 was 1967's fastest Grand Prix car. It also won the 1968 World Constructors Championship.

In 1968 the Ford Company made Cosworth DFV engines available not only to Lotus, but to any racing car builder who could pay for them. Before long nearly

Wings proved more effective without stilts. The front wing of the Lotus Ford 49 became part of the nose-wedge.

1967 Lotus 49

In this Ferrari 312B, the larger rear wing is 'swooped' over the engine between the larger rear tyres.

1970 Ferrari 312B

everyone was using them. The Cosworth DFV has now won over 140 Grands Prix.

In 1970, Ferrari at last produced a rival engine to the Cosworth. This was a horizontally opposed 'boxer' engine with 6 cylinders on each side. It powered the 312B chassis designed by Mauro Forghieri. Jacky Ickx drove the 312B to several Grand Prix victories in 1970.

51

Low Down on the Tracks

In 1965 the French aerospace company, Engins Matra, employed Englishman Ken Tyrrell to develop a racing car for them. In 1967 the French Government and the Elf petrol company gave Matra financial backing to develop a V12 Grand Prix car. In 1969, Matra driver Jackie Stewart won six Grands Prix and the World Championship.

Then, in 1970, Ken Tyrrell decided to develop his own Grand Prix car. The Tyrrell 001 was designed by Derek Gardner and built in the greatest secrecy. During the next two years, Gardner developed the Tyrrell cars with the fantastic driving abilities of drivers Jackie Stewart and Frenchman François Cevert in mind. In 1971 the Tyrrell 003 won six Grands Prix and the World Constructors Championship. Then 005s raced in 1972, and 006s in 1973. When François Cevert was killed in Tyrrell 006/3 in the United States, Jackie Stewart also retired from motor racing. Stewart had won

1973 Tyrrell Ford 006/2

three World Championships and 27 Grands Prix.

The Tyrrells' greatest rival was Colin Chapman's Lotus-Ford 72, which first appeared in 1970. It raced for six Grand Prix seasons. Instead of being in front, the Lotus 72 radiator was at the sides. Its Cosworth-Ford DFV gave 440 bhp at 10,000 rpm. The Lotus 72 had inboard front and rear brakes. Because the Player Cigarette company paid the bills of the Lotus team, its racing cars were painted the colours of their cigarette packets. This is called sponsorship.

The Lotus 72 won three World Constructors Championships and two Drivers Championships for Austrian Jochen Rindt in 1970 and Brazilian Emerson Fittipaldi in 1972.

Jackie Stewart in the Tyrrell Ford 006/2 leading Emerson Fittipaldi in the Lotus 72, in one of their frequent duels during the 1973 season.

1970 Lotus 72

The Mid-1970's

The New Zealander Bruce McLaren died in 1970 testing one of his cars. But his wife and team kept the McLaren name alive on the Grand Prix circuits. The McLaren-Ford M23, designed by Gordon Coppuck, won the 1974 World Constructors Championship. Englishman James Hunt also drove the McLaren 23 to win his 1976 World Drivers Championship.

For ten years, Ferrari had been trying to beat the British. By 1975, their Fiat-12 engine had been developed to give 480 bhp at 12,200 rpm. The new Ferrari 312T – T for transverse gearbox – won the Constructors Championship in 1975, 1976 and 1977.

The McLaren-Ford M23 of 1976; by this time, the single, dominant airbox had been officially banned.

1976 McLaren-Ford M23

Ferrari's Austrian driver, Niki Lauda, also won the Drivers Championship for 1975 and 1977.

Meanwhile, Tyrrell and Gardner had produced the revolutionary P34 six-wheeler. Although four front wheels created less wind resistance, the Tyrrell P34 was not very successful.

1975 Ferrari Fiat 12 312T

The Ferrari Fiat 12 312T of 1975; at this time most Grand Prix cars had tall airboxes to help their engines 'breathe'.

In the Tyrrell Project P34/2, the 1960s slimline look has been replaced by broader aerodynamic shapes.

1976 Tyrrell P34/2

55

Supercharged Revival

Since 1966 the Grand Prix Formula had allowed 3-litre unsupercharged cars and 1½-litre supercharged cars. Most constructors had used the 3-litre unsupercharged engine, like the Ford-Cosworth DFV. In 1977 the Regie-Renault car company, sponsored by the French Government, built a Grand Prix car where the 1½-litre V6 engine was supercharged by an exhaust-driven turbocharger to give 500 bhp. Following two seasons of development, the turbo-charged Renault RS10 was

Ronnie Peterson in the 'ground effect' Lotus 79 and Jean Pierre Jabouille in the turbocharged Renault RS/01 during the 1978 Austrian Grand Prix.

1977 Renault RS01

driven by Frenchman Jean Pierre Jabouille to win the French Grand Prix. A Renault racing car had won the 1906 Grand Prix, but this was the first victory for a supercharged car since 1961.

Colin Chapman also came up with a new Lotus. Having developed the shapes above his cars to give greater speed, he now concentrated on developing shapes underneath and round the bottom of the car. Such shapes included skirts around the side to keep in the airflow. This became known as 'ground effect'. Following the experimental Lotus 78 with flexible skirts in 1977, came the Lotus 79 with rigid skirts in 1978. The Lotus 79, as driven by Italian-born Mario Andretti, and Swedish Ronnie Peterson was another Chapman success story.

1977 Lotus 79

The Eighties

Englishman Frank Williams' first Grand Prix car was completed in 1972 and called a Politoys. His first Williams car appeared in 1975. The Williams FW05 came in 1976. Williams cars have always used the Cosworth DFV engine. From 1978 Williams gained the sponsorship of Saudia Airlines. Thus Williams' Grand Prix car came to be known as the Saudia-Leyland-Williams. It was designed by Patrick Head and aerodynamicist Frank Dearney.

In 1979 Alan Jones, son of Australian racing driver Stan Jones, drove the Saudia-Leyland-Williams FW07 to four Grand Prix victories. But he was beaten to the Championships by South African Jody Scheckter and Canadian Gilles Villeneuve driving Ferrari 312T/4s. In 1980, driving the Williams FW07B, Alan Jones won seven Grands Prix and both World Championships.

Early tyres took a long time to change while racing. The damaged one had to be cut away. Soon after, whole wheel changes became more efficient. While 1950s tyres (centre) were 15 cm wide, today's rear tyres (right) have grown to 46 cm.

58

1980 World Champion Alan Jones makes a lightning pit stop in the Williams FW07B. If it rains, Grand Prix cars change to 'wet' tyres. If the weather improves, they change back to 'dry' tyres.

1980 Williams FW078B

Where to Now?

Today Grand Prix races take place on circuits all over the world. The average length of a circuit is 3-4 miles. Each race lasts for 60-90 laps of the circuit, totalling 180-200 miles (300-320 kilometres). Races last for 90-100 minutes. Cars average 100-120 mph. They do 185 mph on the straights and corner at 160 mph. They are often separated from each other by only fractions of a second. Spectators often number over 100,000, with maybe millions more television viewers. The sport has come a long way from the gruelling races of our grandfathers' day.

1981 Arrows 'prototype'

One way to increase 'ground effect' may be a return to front-engined cars, as in this Arrows prototype.

In 1981, turbocharged cars made the running: the Ferrari 126C-K driven by Villeneuve, the Renault RE 20s, the Brabham-Ford BT 49s with their hydropneumatic suspension. The year 1981 also saw another big step forward by Colin Chapman with his twin-chassis Lotus 88, which was banned by officials, and the

87, which they allowed to race.

Who can tell what tomorrow's racing cars will look like? Grand Prix Formula One rules are always being changed. Designers and constructors must develop new ideas, in accordance with these rules, and with great concern for the safety of their drivers. As cars become increasingly more expensive to build, so raising funds from sponsors wishing to advertise their products on the chassis of the car becomes vital. Perhaps before 1985 racing car speeds will have reached 200 mph.

For Williams, a six-wheeler may be the way to increase 'ground effect'.

1981 Williams 'prototype'

61

Index

63